Contents

Introduction

Developing the skills of adding and subtracting numbers

Children's first steps in learning about adding and subtracting begin informally at home with objects being given and taken away. Later, when they start to handle objects and play with toys they begin to recognize the notion of more or less when something is added or taken away. Young children also begin to recognize that if an object is hidden, something is missing.

By the time children reach four years of age, those of average ability and above are beginning to make links between counting, adding and subtracting by counting small numbers of objects, adding one more or taking one away. They are also starting to draw marks or pictures to represent a number of objects and will know that if they draw a picture of a ball and a brick, for example, that they have drawn 'two'.

This book focuses on developing young children's counting, addition and subtraction skills in a variety of situations. Children are introduced to early addition and subtraction patterns through number rhymes. Number games and practical activities are used to develop children's skills in counting one, then two more or less, combining two groups of objects and counting to find the total, taking objects away and counting how many are left, and early work with double numbers to 5. There are also opportunities throughout the book for children to practise skills of writing numbers to 10 in different situations.

This book follows on from the two counting books *Numbers to 5* and *Numbers to 10* in this series and focuses on making the link between

counting on and addition, and counting back and subtraction. Later activities in the book direct children towards achieving the Early Learning Goals related to addition and subtraction for the Reception year.

Early Learning Goals

The activities in this book are aimed at children who are reasonably confident with counting and writing numbers to 10, and have experience of using numbers in their everyday lives to solve simple problems that involve counting. They are ideal for children who are ready to extend their skills to include simple addition and subtraction of objects and numbers in practical contexts.

The book provides a programme that helps children towards achieving the following Early Learning Goals for Mathematical development, identified by the Qualifications and Curriculum Authority (QCA). This includes:

- count reliably up to 10 everyday objects
- are familiar with counting games, number rhymes, songs and stories
- recognize numerals 1 to 9
- find one more or one less than a number from 1 to 10
- begin to relate addition to combining two groups of objects, and subtraction to 'taking away'
- use developing mathematical ideas and methods to solve practical problems
- through practical activities, record numbers and show an awareness of number operations such as add one more, take one away, how many altogether, how many left?

Baseline Assessment

All of the activities in this book are planned to develop mathematical skills in young children that will enable them to achieve the Early Learning Goals for Mathematical development by the end of the Reception year. This in turn will enable them to confidently tackle the Baseline Assessment Tasks that they will be expected to carry out when they enter Reception classes in mainstream schools.

How to use this book

The activities in this book are designed to be used flexibly according to children's levels of development. While there is a planned structure to the activities for average four-year-olds, consideration is also given to younger and older children with support and extension ideas. This book is specifically designed to offer activities for children to develop their skills in addition and subtraction with numbers to 10. There are structured practical group and individual activities, games focusing on addition and subtraction with numbers to 10 and photocopiable sheets to help children consolidate their skills of adding and subtracting objects and numbers.

Where a photocopiable sheet is to be used by individual children, the activity is referred to as 'Individual recording' and can be kept for assessment purposes. If a sheet is to be used by a group of children, for example a game board, then it is referred to as an 'Individual task'. All the activities are adult directed and require the presence and interaction of an adult.

Where the sheet requires the children to cut out strips of animals/characters, you may prefer to cut off the strips from the photocopiable sheets before the activity, so that the children only have to cut their strips into sections using a one-way cutting action. This enables them to focus on the learning objective rather than the cutting-out process!

The Skills development chart at the back of the book is designed to help you incorporate the activities in your planning procedures. Ensure that adult helpers are pre-briefed about the activities and the preparation that is required beforehand.

Progression

This book takes each number from 5 to 10 in turn as a focus for games and practical activities. It begins with finding numbers that are one more or one less, and combining two small groups of objects with objects and numbers to 5, through number rhymes and familiar everyday contexts. As the book progresses, activities include combining two different groups of objects, taking objects away, simple dice games and activities such as threading beads where children use repeated patterns of adding and subtracting one, then two objects or numbers, and doubling numbers to 5. Children are also given opportunities to work with money and dominoes later in the book.

Finding out what children already know

Before you begin to plan your work, it is helpful to find out what children already know. You can achieve this by:

• finding out how far a child can count orally
• checking how far a child can count objects correctly by touching them and saying the number
• seeing if a child can write numbers in a recognizable form
   • finding out how many objects a child can count by sight without touching them
   • counting out a small set of objects with a child, then adding (taking) one or two objects. Does the child tell you the number by touching and counting the objects or is the child able to work it out mentally?

Home links

Each activity includes suggestions for how parents and carers can help their children at home.

If you wish to involve the support of parents, it is important to establish this principle at the beginning, and ensure that parents receive appropriate guidance. This can be achieved informally through daily contact. If you are concerned about a child and wish parents to help their child with a particular skill, it is important that you share your ideas with the child's parents and invite their observations.

One more/one less

Learning objectives
To add one more object to a set, count and write the total number; to subtract one object from a set, count and write the number left.

Group size
Four to six children working with an adult.

What you need
A copy of the photocopiable sheet for each child for each activity; a tray of different sets of five small objects; a paper plate; pencils; crayons or felt-tipped pens.

What to do
One more: place the paper plate and the tray of objects in the centre of a table. Name a set of objects in the tray, for example 'cubes' and invite a child to take a cube from the tray and put it on the plate. Ask, 'How many cubes on the plate?'. Invite another child to 'put one more cube on the plate' and ask how many there are on the plate again until there are five objects in total. Repeat with another set of objects. Then invite individual children to place different numbers of objects on the plate, for example three beads. Ask, 'How many would be on the plate if there was one more?'. Include an example with no objects on the plate.
One less: repeat the activity in another session, playing the game in reverse taking objects from a plate, asking children to 'Make one less cube on the plate'.

Individual recording
One more: give each child a copy of the photocopiable sheet. Invite them to trace over the numbers at the top of the

sheet starting at the big dots and following the arrows. Ask the children to count the number of objects in each set and write the number in the square. Next, they should draw one more of the objects in the space, count how many altogether and write the number in the circle after the arrow. Finish by colouring the pictures.
One less: repeat the activity in another session with the rule 'One less', where the children cross out one of the objects in each set.

Support
Let the children work through the sheet with you as a group. Ask them to count each set of objects aloud with you. If a child has difficulty writing numbers, scribe them in a yellow marker on the sheet for the child to trace.

Extension
Increase the number of objects used in the oral activity and change the rule to 'Two more' and 'Two less'. Ask the children to draw two more objects on the sheet each time.

Assessment
Check whether the child can count objects by sight or whether he needs to touch and count each object. Can the child add one more/take one away in his head or does he need to recount the objects in ones. Can the child write the numbers on the sheet correctly?

Home links
Encourage parents to help their children by letting them count small sets of objects at home, such as forks or spoons, adding one more to the set or taking one away and saying the number.

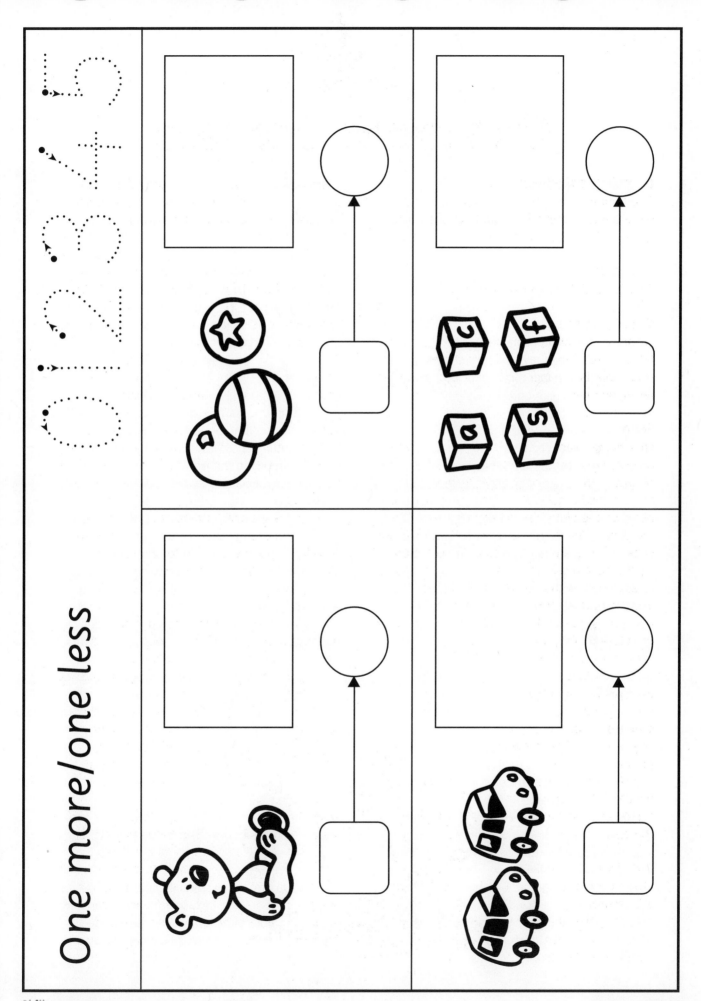

One more/one less

Frogs on a log

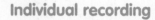

Learning objectives
To sing the song, 'Five Little Speckled Frogs'; count objects to five; subtract different numbers of objects from five and say how many are left.

Group size
Four to six children.

What you need
A copy of the photocopiable sheet for each child; one copy of the sheet enlarged to A3 size on card; a copy of the song 'Five Little Speckled Frogs' from *Apusskidu* (A & C Black); a marker pen; scissors; glue; pencils, crayons or felt-tipped pens.

Preparation
On the large copy of the photocopiable sheet, colour the pool picture and the frogs and then laminate the card. Cut out the picture of the log in the pool and the frog cards. Make a teaching chart on a sheet of paper with two columns headed 'Log' and 'Pool'. Attach it to an easel.

What to do
Sit in a circle and sing the song, 'Five Little Speckled Frogs'. Choose five children to be the frogs sitting on a bench in the centre of the circle. Sing the song again and when you reach the line, 'One jumped into the pool', ask a 'frog' to get off the log and lie down in a space in the circle. Continue throughout the song and repeat with different children.

Display the prepared chart and place the five frog cards along the log on the laminated board. Ask the children in turn to make a frog 'jump into the pool' by taking one from the log and placing it in the pool. Ask, 'How many frogs are left on the log?'; 'How many are in the pool?'. Replace the five frogs on the log and repeat; this time scribe or invite a child to write the numbers in the 'Log' and 'Pool' columns each time.

Individual recording
Give each child a copy of the photocopiable sheet. Ask them to colour the log picture and the frogs then to carefully cut out the frog cards. Invite them to trace over the numbers at the top of the sheet. Ask them to count the number of frog cards they have, and to write the number next to the frog on the right-hand side. Encourage the children to place all the frogs on the log, then to move one into the pool. They can then count how many are left on the log and how many in the pool, writing the numbers on the chart. Finally, they can glue the frogs into the picture choosing how many sit on the log and how many are in the pool.

Support
Ask the children to copy you, placing the frogs on the log or in the pool and to count and say the number of frogs on the log and in the pool.

Extension
Show the log picture and say, 'Let's pretend there are five frogs on the log. If two jump into the pool, how many are left on the log?'.

Assessment
Can the child count how many frogs are on the log or in the pool and write the numbers on the sheet correctly? When asked, 'How many frogs are on the log?' and 'How many frogs are in the pool?', does she need to touch and count each frog or can she count them by sight?

Home links
Ask parents to use two small plates and a set of five or more objects. Tell them to ask their child to put the objects on one plate, then move some to the second plate. Ask, 'How many are left on the first plate?'.

5
4
3
2
1
0

Frogs on a log

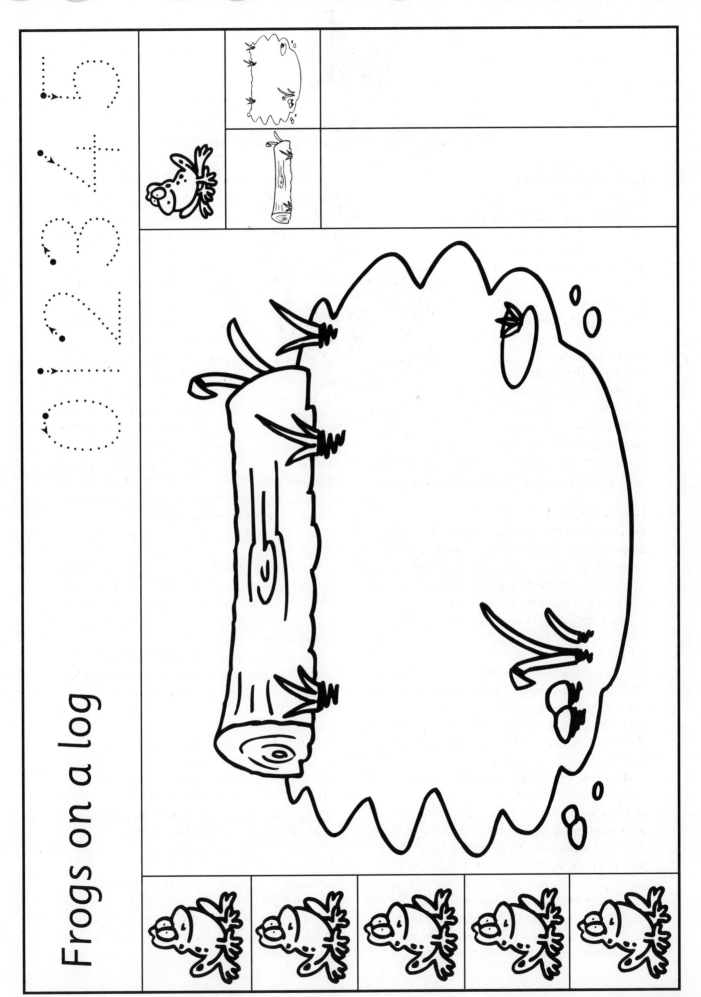

Two more/two less

Learning objectives

To add two more objects to a set, count and write the total number; to subtract two objects from a set, count and write the number left.

Group size

Four to six children working with an adult.

What you need

One copy of the photocopiable sheet for each child for each activity; a set of small toy cars (six or more); a strip of black paper 40cm x 10cm; pencils, crayons or felt-tipped pens.

What to do

Two more: place the strip of paper and the cars in the centre of a table. Tell the children that the strip of paper is a track and that they are going to put cars on the track and count them. Invite a child to take a car from the tray and place it on the track near one end. Ask, 'How many cars are on the track?'. Invite another child to put two more cars on the track and again ask how many cars are on the track. Next take the cars off and ask a child to put two cars on the track with another child putting on two more. Take the cars off then ask for three cars followed by two more, then four and so on, to leave six cars on the track altogether. Then invite individuals to place different numbers of cars on the track, for example three, then ask, 'How many cars would be on the track if there were two more?'. Include an example with no cars on the track.

Two less: repeat the activity in another session with the rule 'Two less' or 'Take two cars away'.

Individual recording

Two more: give each child a copy of the photocopiable sheet. Invite them to trace over the numbers at the top of the sheet. Ask them to count the number of objects in each line and write the number in the square. Next they should draw two more in the space, count how many altogether and write the number in the circle after the arrow.

Two less: repeat the activity in another session with the rule 'Two less' where the children cross out one of the objects in each set.

Support

Let the children work with you as a group, counting each set of objects aloud together.

Extension

Increase the number of objects used in the oral activity and change the rule to 'Three more' and 'Three less'. Ask the children to draw three more objects on the sheet each time.

Assessment

Check whether the child can count objects in their head or whether he needs to touch and count each object. Can the child add two more/ take two away in his head or does he need to recount the objects in ones. Can the child write the numbers on the sheet correctly?

Home links

Encourage parents to let their children place some shoes in a line, adding two more to the line or taking two away and saying the number.

Two more/
two less

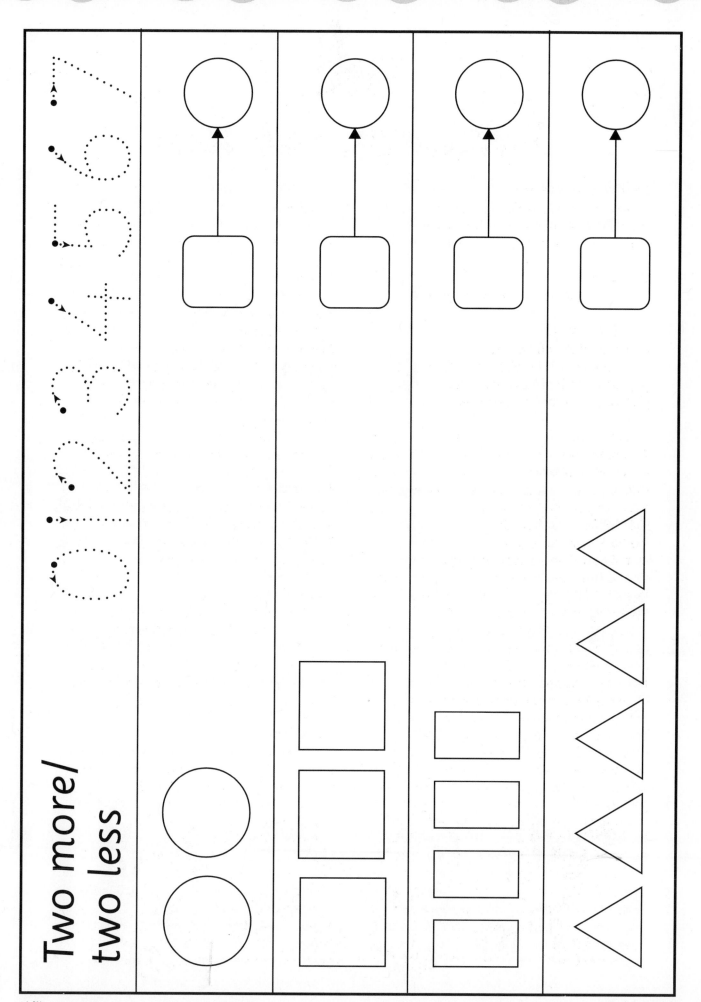

Butterflies and bees

Learning objectives
To count objects to six; add two different sets of objects and say how many of each make six; to begin to recognize pairs of numbers that make six.

Group size
Four to six children working with an adult.

What you need
A copy of the photocopiable sheet for each child; one copy of the sheet enlarged to A3 size on card; a marker pen; scissors; glue; pencils, crayons or felt-tipped pens.

Preparation
Colour the leaf picture, the butterflies and the bees on the enlarged photocopiable sheet and then laminate. Cut out the leaf picture and the butterfly and bee cards. Make a teaching chart on a sheet of paper with two columns headed 'Butterflies' and 'Bees'. Attach it to an easel.

What to do
Place the laminated leaf picture and the butterfly and bee cards face up on the table near the teaching chart. Tell the children that the butterflies and bees can sit on the leaf together but the leaf can only hold six insects at a time. Start by putting one bee on the leaf and inviting the children to take turns to place one butterfly on the leaf counting the number of insects each time until there are six. Then ask, 'How many butterflies are on the leaf?'; 'How many bees?'. Scribe or invite a child to write the numbers in the columns on the chart with the marker pen. Repeat with two bees, then three, up to six.

   Next, invite individual children to put six insects on the leaf using different numbers of bees and butterflies. Write the numbers on the chart each time.

Individual recording
Give each child a copy of the photocopiable sheet and ask them to colour the leaf and the insects, then to carefully cut out the butterfly and bee cards. Ask them to write the number six in the small leaf outline. Encourage the children to place different numbers of bees and butterflies on the leaf to total six, counting how many of each and writing the numbers on the chart each time. When the task is complete ask the children to glue bees and butterflies on the leaf in a way to make six that uses the same number of each insect.

Support
Demonstrate using the laminated leaf picture and insect cards. Ask the children to copy you placing six butterflies on the leaf. Then ask them to change one butterfly for a bee, count them and write the numbers on the sheet.

Extension
Point out that six can be made with pairs of two numbers the same but in a different order for example, 1 and 5; 5 and 1. Can they spot any other pairs? Show the leaf picture and say 'Let's pretend there are four bees on the leaf, how many butterflies are needed to make six?'.

Assessment
Can the child make six using different combinations of bees and butterflies? When asked, 'How many butterflies/ bees?' does she need to touch and count each insect or can she count them by sight? Can the child write the numbers on the sheet correctly?

Home links
Ask parents to use a plate and two different sets of six objects such as pasta shells and buttons. They can ask their child to put six objects on the plate using different combinations of numbers from each set, asking how many of each on the plate and how many objects altogether.

Butterflies and bees

0 1 2 3 4 5 6

Threading beads

Learning objective
To recognize, copy and continue simple numerical sequences of colours and shapes by threading beads.

Group size
Four to six children working with an adult.

What you need
A copy of the photocopiable sheet for each child; a tray containing coloured round and square beads; threading laces; crayons or felt-tipped pens.

What to do
Start by showing the children how to thread a pattern of six beads using beads of two colours or shapes. Point to each bead on the lace and ask the children to say the colour aloud. Then ask them to say the colour and shape of the bead that should be threaded next and thread the bead on for them. Repeat.

Give each child a threading lace and encourage them to each thread six beads on their laces in a pattern using two different-coloured or different-shaped beads. Ask each child to tell you the pattern that they have used, for example, 'red, blue, red, blue'. Then ask the children to continue threading the beads in the same pattern to finish the necklace. Tie the necklaces around each child's neck and let them wear them for the remainder of the session.

Individual recording
Give each child a copy of the photocopiable sheet and ask them to thread one red, round bead and then one blue, round bead on their lace. Then repeat with one more red and blue, round bead. Ask the children to point to each bead on the lace and say the colour aloud. Ask them to say the colour of bead to be threaded next and tell them to thread the bead. Do this again, and then tell the children to copy and continue the pattern by colouring the beads on the first lace on the sheet. Next, tell the children to replace the beads in the tray. Repeat the activity starting with one green, round bead and one yellow, square bead. Repeat again starting with two round beads of one colour and two square beads of another colour.

Support
Ask the children to copy you placing beads on the sheet one at a time on each of the beads shown on the first lace. Then tell the children to colour each bead on the sheet in turn to match, replacing each bead in the tray after they have finished. Repeat with the other two laces on the sheet. When they have finished, ask them to choose one of the bead patterns on the sheet to copy by threading beads on a lace.

Extension
Encourage the children who complete the first activity quickly to thread a necklace in a pattern using beads of three colours or shapes.

Assessment
Note whether the child can thread beads on a lace in a recognizable pattern independently, and whether he can copy and continue given patterns by colouring sets of beads on the sheet.

Home links
Encourage parents to help by using two sets of fruit, for example apples and bananas. Ask them to lay out four pieces of fruit in a line in a pattern, such as 'apple, banana, apple, banana', asking their child to say what comes next and encouraging the child to continue the pattern.

Threading beads

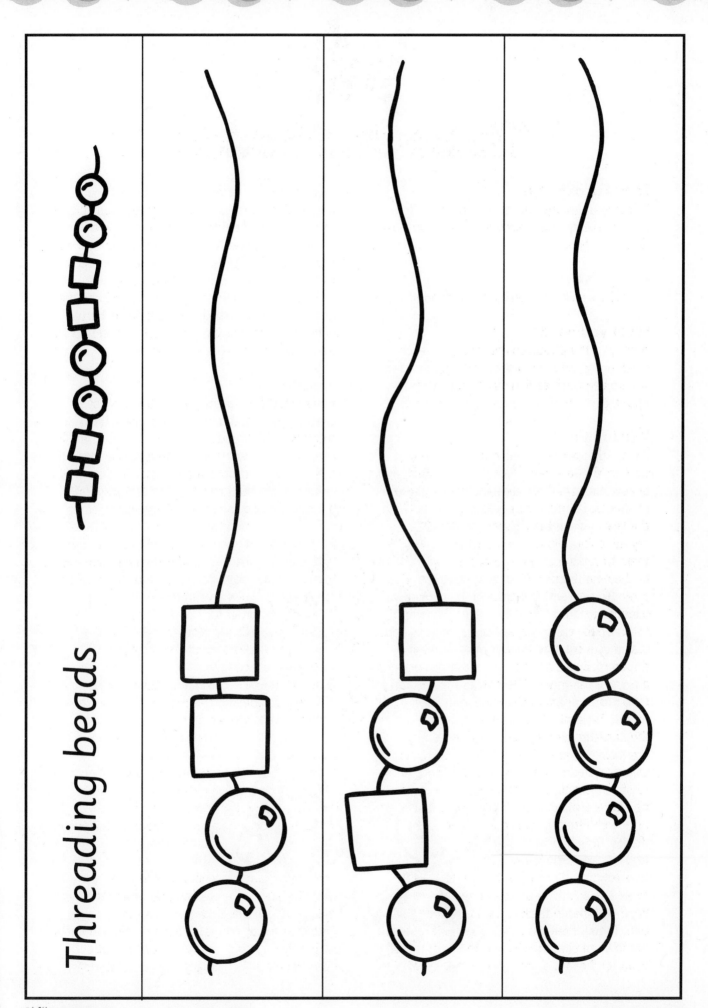

Cars and vans

Learning objectives
To count objects to seven; to add two different sets of objects; to say how many of each make seven.

Group size
Four to six children working with an adult.

What you need
A copy of the photocopiable sheet for each child; one copy of the sheet enlarged to A3 size and copied onto card; a marker pen; scissors; glue; pencils, crayons or felt-tipped pens.

Preparation
Colour the car-park picture and the cars and vans on the enlarged photocopiable sheet and laminate. Cut out the car-park picture and the car and van cards. Make a teaching chart with two columns headed, 'Cars' and 'Vans'.

What to do
Display the teaching chart and place the laminated car-park picture and the car and van cards face up on the table. Tell the children that the car-park has spaces for seven vehicles and that they must find ways to park different numbers of cars and vans in it. Start by asking a child to park one car, then invite the children to take turns to park one van, counting the number of vehicles each time until there are seven in the car-park. Then ask, 'How many cars are there?'; 'How many vans?'. Scribe or invite a child to write the numbers in the columns on the chart using the marker pen. Repeat with two cars, then three, up to seven cars. Then invite individuals to park seven vehicles in the car-park using different numbers of cars and vans.

Individual recording
Give each child a copy of the photocopiable sheet and ask them to colour the cars and vans, then to carefully cut out the car and van cards. Encourage children to park different numbers of cars and vans in the car-park to total seven. Tell them to count how many of each and write the numbers on the chart each time. Finish by gluing cars and vans in the parking spaces so that there is one more van than cars.

Support
Demonstrate the activity using the laminated car-park picture and vehicle cards. Ask the children to copy you parking seven cars in the car-park. Then ask them to drive one car out of the car-park and drive a van in to take its place. Ask them to count the cars and vans and write the numbers on the sheet.

Extension
At the end of the oral activity, ask the children to look at the chart. Point out that seven can be made with pairs of two numbers the same but in a different order for example, 2 and 5; 5 and 2. Can they spot any other pairs?

Assessment
Note whether the child can make seven using different combinations of cars and vans. When a child is asked, 'How many cars?' and 'How many vans?', does she need to touch and count each vehicle or can she count them by sight.

Home links
Ask parents to use a table mat and sets of seven toy cars and vans, inviting their children to park seven vehicles using different combinations from each set. Ask how many of each in the car-park and how many vehicles altogether?

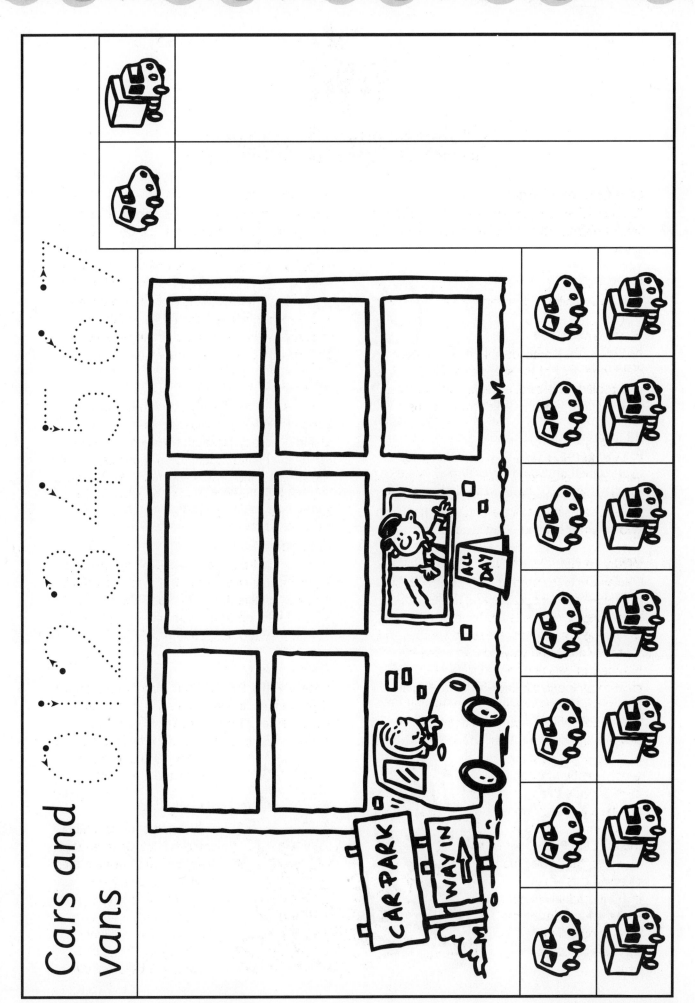

Cars and vans

Eating pizza

Learning objective
To subtract different numbers of objects from eight and say how many are left.

Group size
Game for two to four children working with an adult.

What you need
To make the pizza: pre-prepared pizza base; jar of pizza sauce; grated cheese; slices of tomato, ham, spicy sausage and so on for topping; non-stick baking tray (or microwaveable platter); wooden spoon.
NB Check for allergies and dietary requirements.
For the game: a copy of the photocopiable sheet copied onto card for each player; a dice or cube marked 0, 0, 1, 1, 2, 2; a shaker.

Preparation
Colour each of the pizza cards and laminate them. Cut around each pizza and cut up into the eight pieces. Mark each set of pieces with different-coloured stickers on the back and secure each set with an elastic band.

What to do
Talk about pizzas with the children, asking them to name their favourite toppings. Make a pizza together by spreading the pizza sauce on the base, sprinkling with grated cheese and decorating it with the children's choice of toppings. Cook in a preheated oven according to manufacturer's instructions. Allow the pizza to cool until just warm. Cut the pizza into eight pieces and serve on plates.

Individual task
Tell the children that they are going to play a game called 'Eating pizza'. They must take turns to throw the dice and 'eat' the number of pieces of pizza shown on the dice by taking pieces away each time. The first child to 'eat' all the pizza calls out, 'All gone. Yummy!' and is the winner.

Give each child a set of pizza pieces and ask them to place them together to make a whole pizza. Start the game when everyone has finished putting their pizzas together. During the game, take some time in between turns to ask
• individual children how many pieces of pizza they have left and how many have been 'eaten'.

Support
Help any child who has difficulty making the pizza to start the game. Play the game with a dice marked 1, 1, 1, 0, 0, 0.

Extension
Play the game again in reverse where the children have to build the whole pizza by throwing the dice and placing the number of pieces shown in position. First child to build the whole pizza calls out 'Pizza!' and is the winner.

Assessment
Note whether the child can play the game correctly. When asked to count the pieces of pizza left or eaten, does the child need to touch each piece to count them or can he count them by sight?

Home links
Copy the recipe to give to parents to make a pizza at home with their child and cut it into enough slices for each member of the family.

Eating pizza

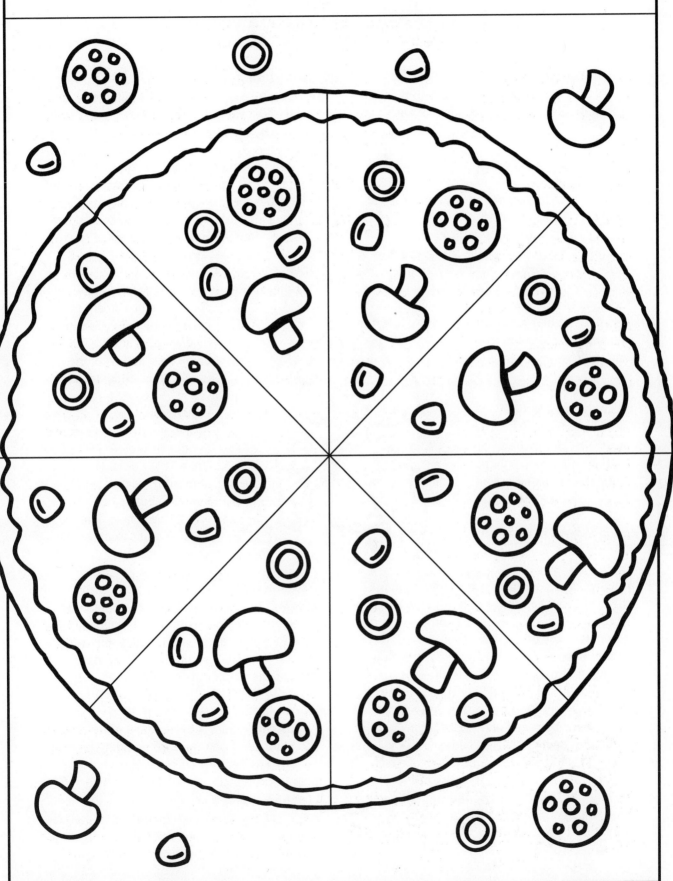

Building towers

Learning objectives
To count objects to eight; to add two different sets of objects and say how many of each make eight; to begin to recognize pairs of numbers that make eight.

Group size
Four to six children working with an adult.

What you need
A copy of the photocopiable sheet for each child; one copy of the sheet for yourself enlarged to A3 size and placed on an easel; red, blue and black marker pens; sets of eight blue and eight red interlocking cubes; blue and red crayons.

What to do
Place the enlarged photocopiable sheet where everyone can see it and give each child a set of eight red and eight blue interlocking cubes. Tell the children to make a tower of eight cubes using red and blue cubes. Choose individual children to show their tower and say the number of red and blue cubes used, then ask them to copy their tower using the marker pens to colour squares on the chart and to write the numbers in the boxes underneath their tower. Repeat until all the towers have been coloured. (Ensure that each tower shows different combinations of red and blue cubes.) Point to each tower on the sheet in turn and ask, 'How many red cubes are there?'; 'How many blue cubes are there?'.Can the children show you the set of two numbers the same that make eight?

   Remove the sheet and then ask questions such as, 'If a tower has two red cubes, how many blue cubes are needed to make a tower of eight?'. Let the children use their cubes to check if they are not sure.

Individual recording
Give each child a copy of the photocopiable sheet and invite them to trace over the numbers at the top, starting at the big dots and following the arrows. Tell the children to build a tower of red and blue cubes, colour the tower they make on the sheet, then to count how many red and blue cubes they have used and write the numbers underneath as they have been shown. Make different towers to complete the sheet.

Support
Ask the children to make a tower of eight red cubes. Then ask them to change one red cube for a blue cube, count the red and blue cubes and write the numbers on the sheet.

Extension
At the end of the oral activity ask the children to look at the chart. Ask individual children to point to pairs of numbers the same but in a different order for example, 2 and 6; 6 and 2. What can they tell you about 4 and 4?

Assessment
Note whether the child can make eight using different combinations of blue and red cubes. When a child is asked, 'How many red/blue cubes?' does she need to touch and count each cube or can she count them by sight?

Home links
Ask parents to play a hiding game using a tub and eight small objects, such as eight 1p coins. Tell them to ask their child to count the coins then to close their eyes while one is hidden under the tub. The child is asked to count the coins again, and say how many coins are under the tub to make the number up to eight. The child checks by looking under the tub.

Building towers

8 7 6 5 4 3 2 1 0

	blue	red
	☐	☐

	blue	red
	☐	☐

	blue	red
	☐	☐

	blue	red
	☐	☐

Knock down nine pins

Learning objectives
To count nine objects; to take different numbers of objects away and find how many are left.

Group size
Four to six children working with an adult.

What you need
A copy of the photocopiable sheet for each child; one copy of the sheet enlarged to A3 size; nine plastic skittles; a plastic ball; a cane; score chart; marker pen; pencils, crayons.

Preparation
Copy the following score chart onto a flip chart:

Name Robin April	Knocked down	Left

Clear a space and set up the skittles. Measure about 4m from the skittles and place the cane to mark the starting line. Sit the children each side of the skittle alley and place the score chart beside the starting line where everyone can see.

What to do
Demonstrate how to stand behind the line and roll the ball to try to knock the skittles down. Ask the children to count how many skittles you knock down and how many are left standing. Then invite one of the children to try the game. Choose a child sitting down to count and say the number of skittles knocked down. The child who rolled the ball writes the number in the 'Knocked down' column on the chart. Ask another child sitting down to count and say the number of skittles left standing. The child who rolled the ball writes the number in the 'Left' column of the chart. Let each child have a turn.

Look at the scores on the chart, asking the children to say

how many skittles each child knocked down and how many skittles are left standing each time. Who knocked the most/least skittles down?

Individual recording
Use the enlarged copy of the photocopiable sheet to demonstrate how the children can colour one skittle and then point to each of the 'white' skittles, while the other children count aloud. Ask them to tell you how many are left white and write the number in the first box on the sheet. Repeat by colouring another skittle and so on. Give each child a copy of the photocopiable sheet and tell the children to complete it as they have been shown, colouring one skittle then two and so on until all the skittles are coloured and the chart is complete.

Support
Use the enlarged photocopiable sheet for the children to copy you colouring the skittles on their sheet each time. Ask the children to count the 'white' skittles aloud with you each time and to write the numbers on the chart.

Extension
Ask individual children to point to pairs of numbers on the chart on their sheet that are the same but in a different order for example, 1 and 8; 8 and 1.

Assessment
Note whether the child can count how many skittles have been knocked down each time and how many are left standing. Does he need to touch and count each skittle or can he count them by sight?

Home links
Ask parents to play a game of skittles with their children using a skittles set or a set of plastic bottles and a small ball, and count how many the children knock down.

Knock down nine pins

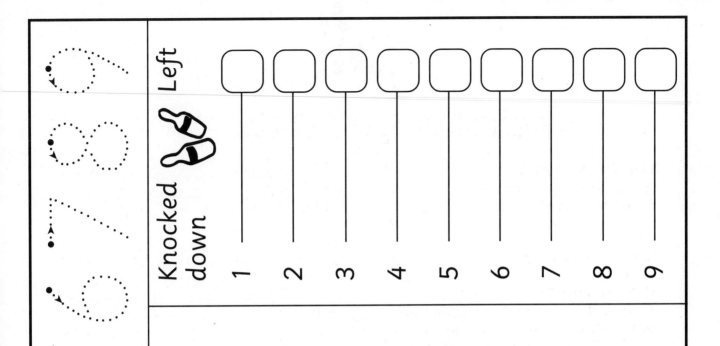

1 2 3 4 5 6 7 8

Knocked down

Left

1	
2	
3	
4	
5	
6	
7	
8	
9	

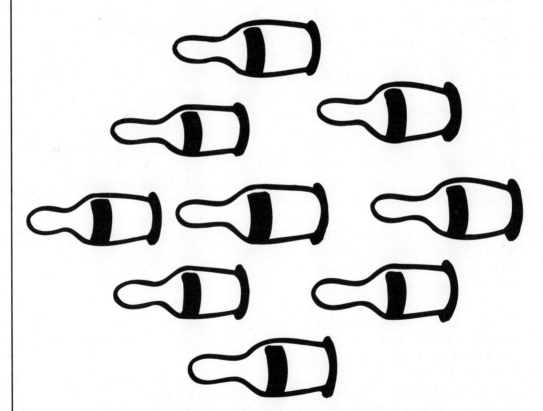

Cows and sheep

Learning objectives
To count objects to ten; to add two different sets of objects and say how many of each make ten; to begin to recognize pairs of numbers that make ten.

Group size
Four to six children.

What you need
A copy of the photocopiable sheet for each child; a large piece of green material or sheet of green paper (pretend field); sets of ten toy cows and sheep; a marker pen; scissors; glue; pencils; colouring materials.

Preparation
Make a teaching chart with two columns headed 'Cows' and 'Sheep'.

What to do
Ask the children to sit in a circle. Place the teaching chart where everyone can see it. Place the pretend field in the middle of the circle and the toy cows and sheep around the outside. Tell the children that the cows and sheep share the field but there is only enough grass for ten animals at a time. Invite a child to put one cow in the field and ask other children to take turns to place one sheep in the field, counting the number of animals each time until there are ten in the field. Then ask, 'How many cows/sheep are in the field?'. Invite a child to write the numbers in the columns on the chart with the marker pen. Repeat up to ten. Then invite a child to put ten animals in the field using different numbers of cows and sheep.

Individual recording
Give each child a copy of the photocopiable sheet. Ask them to colour the field then to carefully cut out the cow and sheep cards. Encourage the children to place different numbers of cows and sheep in the field to total ten. Tell them to count how many of each and write the numbers on the chart. Finish by gluing the cows and sheep in the field to make ten, using the same number of each animal.

Support
Ask the children to place ten cows in the field. Then ask them to change one cow for a sheep, count the cows and sheep and write the numbers on the sheet. Ask them to change another cow for a sheep and so on.

Extension
Ask the children to look at the chart and invite individual children to point to pairs of numbers the same but in a different order for example, 7 and 3; 3 and 7. Can they point to a pair with the same numbers? (5 and 5.)

Assessment
Note whether the child can make ten using different combinations of cows and sheep. When a child is asked, 'How many sheep?' and 'How many cows?', does she need to touch and count each animal or can she count them by sight? Can she show you the set of two numbers the same that make ten?

Home links
Ask parents to play a game using a box with a lid and ten washing pegs. Tell them to ask their child to count the pegs, then to close their eyes while the parent puts one in the box and closes the lid. The child is asked to count the pegs again and say how many pegs are in the box to make the number up to ten. The child counts the pegs in the box to see if they were right.

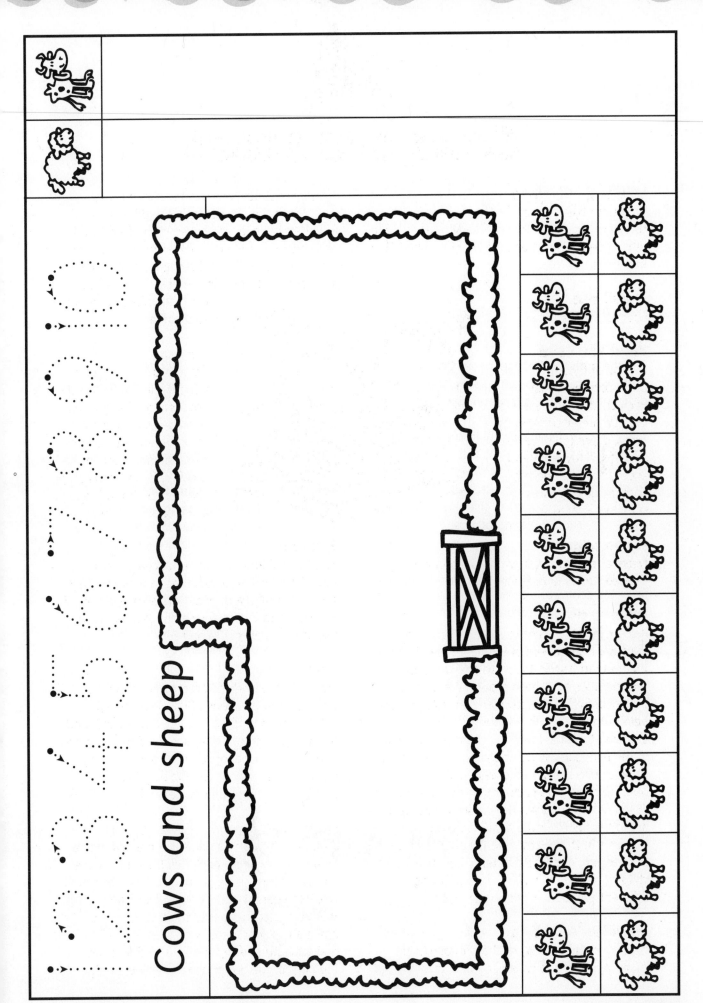

Cows and sheep

Moneybags game

Learning objectives

To count amounts of 1p coins up to 10p; to pay for toys and count how much money is left; to begin to recognize different pairs of numbers that make 10.

Group size

Five children working with an adult.

What you need

For the activity: ten paper plates each marked 1p to 10p; five unmarked paper plates; ten different small toys; a tray containing 1p coins.
For the game: five copies of the photocopiable sheet on card; laminating materials; a tray of 1p coins; a dice marked 0, 0, 1, 1, 2 , 2.

Preparation

Laminate the five copies of the photocopiable sheet to make five playing boards.

What to do

Place five of the plates marked 1p, 3p, 5p, 7p, 9p in the centre of a table and place a small toy on each plate. Give each child an unmarked plate. Ask them to each take ten 1p coins from the tray and place them on the plate. Then ask the children to look at the marked plates and tell you how much each toy costs. Invite each child in turn to choose one of the toys to buy and pay for using their 1p coins. Ask them to put the correct amount of money on the marked plate and take the toy. Ask, 'How much did it cost?' and 'How much money do you have left?'. Collect in the toys and the money on the marked plates, then ask the children to take coins from the tray to make up the coins on their own plate to 10p again. Repeat the activity using the five remaining plates and toys.

Individual task

Give each child a copy of the photocopiable sheet and ten 1p coins. Explain to the children that they can take turns to throw the dice and place the number of coins in the circles on the sheet, according to the number shown on the dice. The first child to have ten coins on their sheet calls out 'Moneybags!' and is the winner.

Support

Carry out the activity with five toys and five plates marked 1p, 2p, 3p, 4p, 5p and give each child five 1p coins.

Extension

Play the moneybags game backwards where the children start by placing ten coins on the coin outlines on the sheet. When they throw the dice they have to take off that number of coins each time. The first child with no coins left on the sheet calls out 'Broke!' and is the winner.

Assessment

Note whether the child can count out ten 1p coins, place the correct amount of money on a plate and say how much money he has left on his plate. Can the child add more coins to his plate to make 10p? In the game, when he is asked, 'How many are on the sheet?' and 'How many are left?', does he need to touch and count each coin or can he count them by sight?

Home links

Ask parents to play a game using a paper bag and ten 1p coins. Their child counts the coins then closes their eyes while the parent puts one in the bag. The child counts the coins again and says how many coins are in the bag to make the number up to ten. The child checks by counting the coins in the bag.

Moneybags game

Doubling numbers

Learning objectives
To recognize double numbers up to six; to add the numbers together to find the total.

Group size
Four children working with an adult.

What you need
A copy of the photocopiable sheet for each child; a set of playing cards; a dice; shaker; a small tub for each child; pencils and crayons.

Preparation
Make a teaching chart by enlarging a copy of the photocopiable sheet to A3 size. Sort out all the aces to sixes from the pack of playing cards and discard the rest. Split the suits into two sets; one containing aces to sixes in diamonds and clubs, the other containing aces to sixes in hearts and spades.

What to do
Show the children some double numbers using sets of two cards with the same number of spots. Then show the children how to find the total by asking them to count the number of spots on one card and say the number, then you point to each spot on the second card for the children to count on from the number in ones.

Spread out the set of hearts and spades cards face up on the table and shuffle the pile of diamonds and clubs. Tell the children that you will give them each a card in turn and that they have to find a card on the table with the same number of spots, pick it up and add the number of spots on the two cards together, saying the total. When they have done that they keep the two cards and play passes to the next child. Repeat with the other two suits.

Individual task
Give each child a copy of the photocopiable sheet, a dice, shaker and a tub. Show the children how to throw the dice in the tub, count the spots and then draw in the spots on the first two dice on the sheet using a crayon to show the number doubled. Next, they should find the total of the two dice and write it in the circle after the arrow. Then, they throw the dice again and so on until they have completed the sheet. If they throw a number they have already used, they must throw again.

Support
Make a master copy of the sheet, drawing in the spots on the first dice in each pair in order of one to six. Ask the children to draw the same number of spots on the second dice and then count how many altogether each time.

Extension
Using a dice numbered one to six, ask the children to work in their heads, use their fingers or interlocking cubes to find the total of the pair of numbers.

Assessment
Note whether the child can recognize double numbers up to six and add the two numbers together to find the total. Note whether she needs to touch and count each spot on the two cards or dice to find the total or whether she can count on in ones from the first number. Are there any double numbers that she can add together by sight?

Home links
Ask parents to help at home by throwing two dice and asking their child to add the two numbers together. Encourage them to play games with their children which use dice.

Doubling numbers

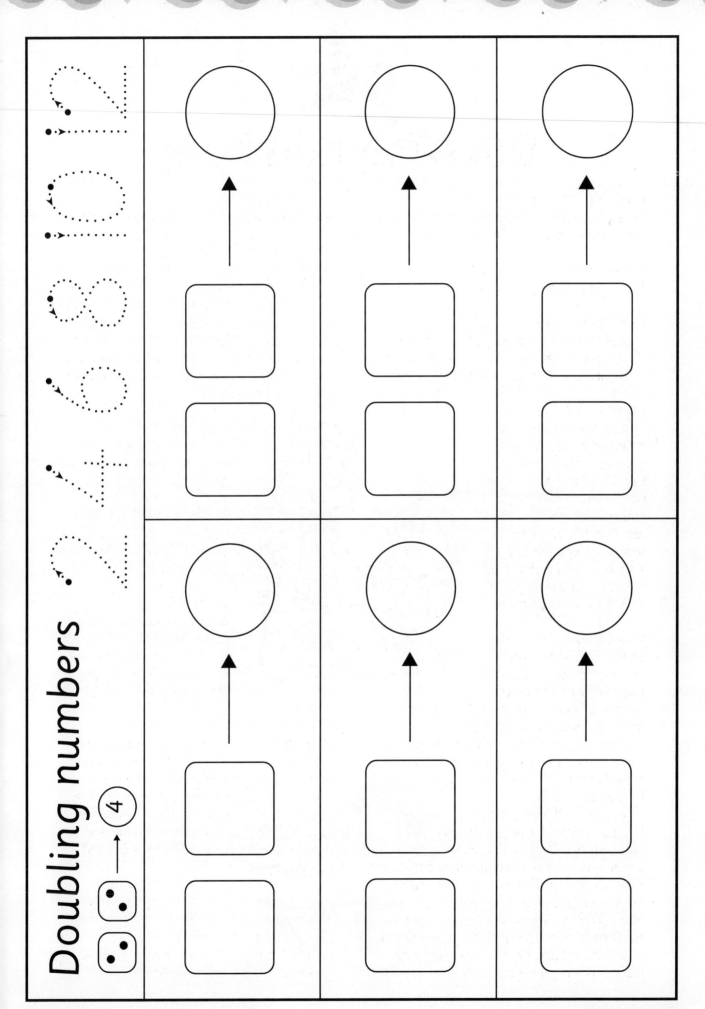

Domino sums

Learning objective
To add two numbers together using the numbers zero to six and find the total.

Group size
Four to six children working with an adult.

What you need
A copy of the photocopiable sheet for each child; a copy of the photocopiable sheet enlarged to A3 size; a set of dominoes; crayons and pencils; a small easel; a marker pen.

Preparation
Attach the enlarged A3 sheet to the easel.

What to do
Lay out all the dominoes face down on the table. Demonstrate by holding up a domino and show the children how to find the total, by asking them to count the number of spots on one half of the domino and say the number, then point to each spot on the second half for the children to count on from the number in ones. Repeat this, asking the children to copy you holding up their fingers to show the number on the first half of the domino, then to count on the second number in ones using fingers. Include an example where one side of a domino is blank. Now ask each child to pick up a domino. Tell the children that you will ask them each in turn to find the total number of spots on the domino using the finger method. Offer guidance to any child who is unsure. Continue until there are no dominoes left.

Individual recording
Display the enlarged photocopiable sheet and lay out all the dominoes face down on the table. Invite a child to pick up a domino and draw the spots on the first domino on the

sheet, then to count and write the number of spots in each half in the boxes underneath. Encourage the child to find the total number of spots by using the finger method or by counting on the spots in the second half of the domino in ones. Tell the child to write the total number in the circle beside the domino. Let each child have a turn to use the sheet. Give each child a copy of the photocopiable sheet and ask them to carry out the activity, as they have been shown.

Support
Use only the dominoes that have spots totalling five or less. If the children are unsure of the counting-on method, encourage them to touch and count each spot.

Extension
Encourage the children to work out any 'easy' addition (adding 0, 1 or 2) in their heads, rather than using a counting-on method. If they can do this, ask them to colour the smiley face beside the domino each time.

Assessment
Note whether the child has copied the spots and numbers correctly on to the sheet and whether he is able to write the total number correctly. Note which numbers the child adds together by using a counting-on method (fingers or spots) and which numbers he is able to add together in his head.

Home links
Ask parents to help their child draw around domino shapes on a sheet of paper, draw in the spots and write the total number of spots beside each domino. Explain how to encourage their children to add the numbers together by using a counting-on method (fingers or spots).

Domino sums

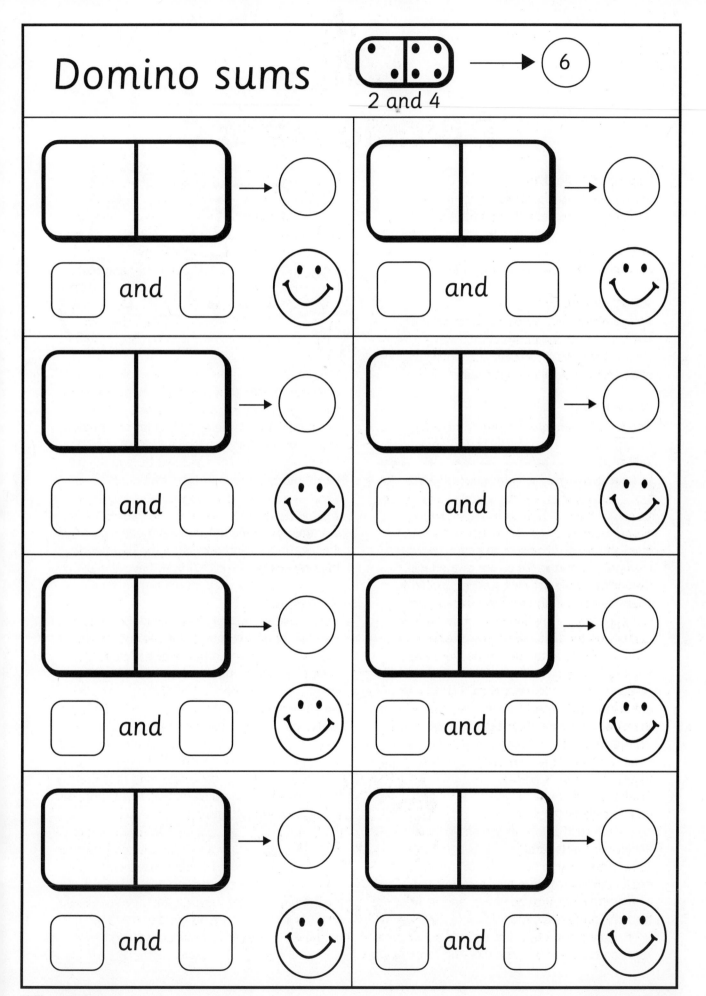

2 and 4 → 6

and

and

and

and

and

and

and

and

Take away game

Learning objective
To count 12 objects, take away different numbers and record how many are left.

Group size
Four to six children working with an adult.

What you need
A copy of the photocopiable sheet for each child; set of 12 objects in a tray; two dice, a shaker and a tub for each child; pencils; large sheet of paper; easel; a marker pen.

Preparation
Copy the following score chart onto a flip chart or large sheet of paper attached to an easel.

Take away	Left

What to do
Place the set of 12 objects in a tray, two dice, shaker and a tub in the centre of the table. Demonstrate the activity by asking a child to throw the dice in the tub, add the numbers together using a counting-on method (fingers or spots) and say the score on the dice. Ask the child to write the number in the 'Take away' column on the score chart. Ask another child to take that number of objects out of the tray, count how many are left and write the number in the 'Left' column on the chart. Replace the objects in the tray. Repeat until every child has taken a turn at throwing the dice or taking the objects from the tray.

Individual recording
Give each child a copy of the photocopiable sheet, two spotty dice, a shaker and a tub. Ask them to colour the balls, then to carefully cut out the ball cards. Ask them to count the number of ball cards they have, and to write the number in the ball outline.

Start by placing the 12 ball cards in the space on the sheet, throwing the dice and carrying out the activity, taking the number of balls shown by the score on the dice off the sheet, and writing the numbers on the chart each time. Tell the children to throw the dice six times to complete the sheet. If a throw is repeated, they should throw again. Invite the children to glue the ball cards into the space on the sheet.

Support
Use only six of the ball cards and one dice. Throw the dice and take away the number of balls shown on the dice. If they have already used the number, they should throw again.

Extension
Use sets of dice numbered one to six. Encourage the children to work out the dice score using their fingers or in their heads where they can.

Assessment
Note whether the child can add the score on two dice correctly using a counting-on method, a 'head' method, or does she still need to touch and count all the spots to find the total? Can the child take that number away and count how many balls are left correctly?

Home links
Ask parents to repeat the first activity at home, using a set of 12 objects and two dice. Explain to the parents that they should encourage their child to add the score on the dice using a counting-on method (fingers or spots) or work the total out in their heads.